Dedication

This book is dedicated to all those with disabilities who are dreaming of an elite and prestigious career. There are no limits! Go for it!!

This book is also dedicated to Pat Price the love of my life: a man who lives his life with honor, courage, determination, and bravery. Pat, you have shown me more love than I have ever known and I will love you forever!

In Memory of Nancy Theis

The best boss and confidant at the
White House.

"Dinner tonight, Katie?"

My first day working at the White House I did not even think about having one arm. I saw the American flag outside the White House and thought this is what it means to follow a dream.

When I first walked inside, the Secret Service asked for my identification and gave me a shiny badge. They even helped me put my coat and bag through the metal detector and camera clearance.

The gold elevators and fancy marble floor reminded me this was no ordinary day.

As the elevator opened I was greeted by my boss Nancy. She had on rectangle glasses, a bob haircut, and a bright pink suit fit for a press conference.

"Welcome to the Office of Presidential Correspondence, Katie!"

After the whirlwind tour of the office, things moved quickly with getting right to work.

Nancy said,
"Ms. Wells, here in the Office of Presidential Correspondence you will have a very important role of answering the phone lines and helping our fellow Americans."

I was not sure how I would hold the phone and write my reports at the same time with one arm, so I was grateful when I saw my desk had a headset.

People called the White House to ask for all types of help from the President with hardship cases, family assistance, medical issues, veterans support, and everyday challenges. It was rewarding helping our fellow Americans.

Nancy would often walk by our desks after a long hard day and say, "Dinner, tonight?"

We were invited to her house for the most lavish of dinner parties with fresh flowers, candlelight, a piano player, and the best dinner and company.

Sometimes my friends and I would explore Washington, D.C. During the winter, we figure skated on the outdoor rink outside the Sculpture Garden at the National Gallery of Art.

On the metro ride to go see the Cherry Blossoms, the disabled seating was filled with patrons without disabilities. With one arm, I could not stand and hold on safely, so I had to ask for someone to give up their seat.

On one particular day, we stayed at work until the late hours to help answer the phones and manage a national crisis. I felt proud to be an American in this important role.

Sometimes my hand and arm hurt from writing and typing up the phone call reports for the President. My boss had the perfect solution and started helping me with the typing! We worked as a team.

When hearing impaired callers called in, it was amazing being able to communicate through the TTY, which allowed the communications to be typed into a screen.

When wounded veterans called the Correspondence office about the challenges they faced with limb loss, I felt proud to help them since I understood what it was like to have one arm.

Helping wounded veterans became very important to me as I saw having one arm as a way to help others. I became a military peer visitor at Walter Reed Army Medical Center and helped the soldiers with limb loss with their recovery on Ward 58 and Ward 57.

One time President Bush came by the office to thank us for our service. I told him that I did peer visiting for the injured soldiers at Walter Reed Army Medical Center. I was so overcome with emotion at sharing this that I cried. The President gave me a kiss on the cheek, a pat on the back, then whispered in my ear, "Keep up the good work!"

I am a champion! I can work at the White House with one arm and so can you!
What is your dream?

The End.

ABOUT THE AUTHOR

Katie Laurel Wells is a U.S. Paralympic swimmer and has competed both nationally and internationally. She competed at the USA National Championships twice, the World Team Trials, and is the silver medalist in the 200 meter breaststroke at the 2004 Paralympic Swimming Trials. In her free time, Katie advocates for those with disabilities and helps veterans, especially those with limb loss with their recovery. Katie is a Certified Peer Visitor through the Amputee Coalition of America. Katie is also the author of the book **I Can Still Do Everything with One Arm.**

For questions or to book speaking engagements please contact: wells.katie@yahoo.com
To read more of Katie's writing please visit: wellslaurel.wordpress.com

ABOUT THE ILLUSTRATOR

Frank Carroll is an artist who focuses on exploring the visual and emotional connections between painting and music. The different sounds, and styles of musical creativity affect the way he paints. Frank has a lifelong pursuit of conveying the structure, color, and soul of the music he paints. Using acrylic, foam core, and canvas, his belief is that a song, album, or style of music could be brought to a visual medium, and could be felt and understood. With acrylic, canvas, and layers of acrylic sheeting, he not only is able to set the tone and visual of the painting, but also now adds dimension and depth to the pieces, further delving into bringing a tangible conception to a sonic world. Special thanks to Robin Jackson Caddell for her inspiration and support. Thank you to Susan Carroll and Emily Hayes for helping this color blind artist pick the perfect palate!

To contact Frank or to learn more about his art please visit: frankcarrollartist.com

Katie and Frank's paths both crossed while working for Blue Ridge Mountain Sports and the two have been lifelong friends ever since.

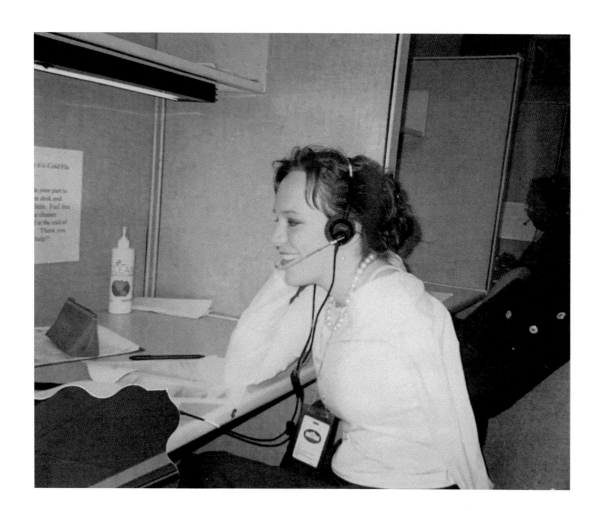

Made in the USA
Columbia, SC
19 April 2023

15328380R00024